THE ROOKS OF TRELAWNE

Andrew Lanyon

Published by The Photographers Gallery
Gordon Fraser Gallery Ltd
Mathews Miller Dunbar

'In one moment I've seen what has hitherto been
Enveloped in absolute mystery,
And without extra charge I will give you at large
A lesson in Natural History.'

The Hunting of the Snark, Lewis Carroll.

Images on the front and back covers and pages 12, 14, 17, 20, 24, 25, 26, 35, 39 and 63 have been prepared for this publication by the author.

Book design and typography by Andrew Lanyon with Roy Walker MSIA

Published by The Photographer's Gallery in association with Gordon Fraser Gallery Ltd and Mathews Miller Dunbar.

Produced by Mathews Miller Dunbar, 51 Endell Street, London WC2H 9AJ.

First Printing
ISBN No. 0 903811 23 5
Photographs Copyright © 1976 Andrew Lanyon.
Text Copyright © 1976 Andrew Lanyon.

Printed by CTD, Twickenham, England.

Distributed by Idea Books.
UK Idea Books/Gordon Fraser, 49 Endell Street, London WC2H 9AJ.
Idea Books Australia, 104 Sussex Street, Sydney 2000, NSW, Australia.
Idea Books Amsterdam, Nieuwe Herengracht 35, Amsterdam, Holland.
Idea Books Paris, 46—48 Rue de Montreuil, 75011 Paris, France.
Idea Books Milan, Via Cappuccio 21, 20123 Milano, Italy.

Acknowledgements

Of the many people who have helped in various ways I should like to thank the following:

Dr. Frank and Stella Turk; Jacqie Levin; Sheila Lanyon; Miss Foy Quiller-Couch; Sheila de Burlet; Sue Davies; Judy Brooks; Mr. Douch; Clive Carter; Mr. W.T. Harry; Mrs. Ruby Saunders; Roger Penhallurick; Mr. Grimes of the Nature Conservancy Council; Brian Court-Mappin; Hubert Chesshyre; Douglas and Dulcie Puckey; Alwyne Wheeler; Arthur Rag; Mary Wright; Mrs. F.E.K. Perrycoste; The Mother Abbess, Sclerder Abbey; Hedley Libby; John Fitzgerald; Lady Mander; Dicon Nance; John Davies; The Rev. William Rowett; Chuck Evans; Professor Charles Thomas; Peter Pool; Charles Harris; Simon Trelawny; Jean and Catherine Gimpel; John and Peter Schofield; Anna Thew and Martin Lugg; Mike Hayes; Eugene Ankeny; Betty Ralph; Rémy Aquarone; Dr. Anthony Michaelis and Mr. Raddy of Looe.

Most of Harding's photographs by permission of The Royal Institution of Cornwall.

Most of the text and pictures on composite photography by permission of The Galton Laboratory.

The etching of William Yarrell by permission of The Linnean Society.

The three calotypes by J.D. Llewelyn by permission of The Royal Photographic Society of Great Britain.

The Polperro view without a fishwife by Francis Frith by permission of Photographic Collections Ltd.

The photograph of a hide by permission of The National Collection of Nature Photographs, copyright E. Hosking, F.R.P.S.

Excerpts on and by Frank Sutcliffe from *Frank Sutcliffe* by Michael Hiley (1974) by permission of Gordon Fraser.

Excerpt from *The Leaping Hare* by G.E. Evans and D. Thomson by permission of Faber and Faber.

Excerpt from *Night's Black Angels* by Ronald Pearsall by permission of Hodder and Stoughton.

Several portraits of Jonathan Couch and excerpts from a manuscript version of his *History of British Fishes* by permission of the Morrab Garden Library, Penzance.

A portrait of Couch by permission of the Cornwall County Library.

THE ROOKS OF TRELAWNE

In 1762 John Wesley described the Cornish fishing village of Polperro as 'surrounded with huge mountains', perhaps an excusable exaggeration from someone arriving on horseback, but Thomas Quiller-Couch's description of 1871, in which he refers to 'tall hills', is more realistic. The century dividing these two men saw hardly any change in Polperro's landward isolation. It was among the smallest and remotest of all Cornish fishing villages and yet produced an unusual number of outstanding men.

In 1856 Jonathan Couch, the local doctor and an eminent naturalist, completed a history of Polperro which was edited for publication by his son Thomas in 1871. Fortunately there exists a handwritten version of this which has pasted into it many of Cornwall's earliest photographs. The curious thing is that nowhere does anyone mention who took them. Although Jonathan Couch, his sons Richard and Thomas, his daughter Bertha and his grandson Sir Arthur all wrote a good deal, nowhere do they mention a photographer. This is especially strange since he must have been well known to all or most of them — there are at least seven pictures of Jonathan and probably two each of Richard and Thomas.

The first thing in the search for the identity of the photographer was to establish the dates of the photographs, hoping to determine when the first and last pictures were taken, and so get some idea of when he was working. A search in Somerset House revealed the birth dates of four children identified in the portraits. From their apparent ages it seemed the pictures were taken in the early 1860's. The telephone directory led to the Vicar of Madron, whose family name of Rowett was common in Polperro. He possessed a family tree, which put the Hannah Rowett portrait at about 1865, and his sister had a photograph of some Rowetts in Polperro harbour, which could be dated to about 1861. Another photograph shows a view of Polperro before the building of 'The Duke of Cornwall' pier in 1861 and of the seven portraits of Jonathan, several show him at least ten years before he died in 1870.

From the portrait of a gentleman (opposite), Dr. Turk deduced the following: 'The fish is a Trunk or Coffer fish from tropical waters and a prized specimen for a 'cabinet of curiosities' such as was beloved of erudite gents from the late 17th to the mid-19th century and later. The bottles are typical 'physic phials' of the period 1830-1880 and he appears to hold an early form of the mono aural stethoscope such as was in common use up to about the 1880's. The man's age is difficult to judge but he looks as though he has had some considerable ill health and has certainly recently had his teeth out — perhaps completely. The broad button-over reefer jacket and the waistcoat with reverses are typical of the period 1857-1865, as is the bow. The only man I can think of who fits all these characteristics and had an interest in fish and was a doctor, was Richard Quiller-Couch (1816-1863). He died aged 47, after pneumonia and a series of incidents of previous ill-health.'

This then is very probably Richard in about 1862. There are no paintings of him to substantiate this, but since every photograph in the *History of Polperro* manuscript is of Polperro or the immediate neighbourhood we can be fairly sure it is of someone local, and therefore almost certainly Richard.

Melanie Barrett   Jane Ann Libby, b.1855

Richard Quiller Couch

In 1854 Richard mentioned the capture of a Thrasher shark at Penzance, where he was living, and since this was far from an everyday occurrence, it could well be the same shark as in the Polperro photograph, brought round by boat for Jonathan to draw and dissect. Jonathan, whose life work *The History of the Fishes of the British Islands* was published in four volumes between 1860 and 1865, had already drawn a Thrasher shark captured at the entrance to Looe harbour in 1826. So unfortunately he had no need to record the date of this second specimen. The two men in the picture who stand out from the others because of their dress could be Thomas and Richard. Richard, the figure pointing, might well be instructing a fisherman to collect water from the stream in order to keep the shark wet. This was important to Jonathan who had constructed a device which played a jet of water over a fish as he painted it, so he could portray it in its true colours. The respective ages of Richard and Thomas (standing behind the cart) in 1854, of 38 and 28, could fit.

All the photographs seem then to have been taken between the early 1850's and late 1870's. Assuming they were the work of one man, we can turn again to the question of who took them. Both Jonathan (died 1870) and Richard (died 1863) can be ruled out. Thomas, however, was a doctor in nearby Bodmin and often visited his father in Polperro. We know he had an interest in painting for although 'his presence in a sick-chamber filled it with a confidence that was half a cure' it was said of him that he was surer with the brush than the scalpel. He edited his father's *History of Polperro* and it was probably he who pasted the photographs into the handwritten version. However, his grand-daughter, Miss Foy Quiller-Couch, thought he had never taken photographs. Early photographers needed so much equipment that some of it nearly always survives. Apart from the chemicals, bottles, lenses, cameras, prints and plates there would have been books and it is strange that not a single one survived with a family, whose life had been books for four generations. A third son, Jonathan, also a doctor in Bodmin, was another possibility, but very little is known about him.

The search for the photographer was helped by Douglas Puckey who remembered his father had said the photographer was not from Polperro and that he may have been from London. It is unlikely he would have been a visitor because Polperro in the 1850's was very poor and one of Cornwall's most isolated fishing villages. Even the artists, who usually paved the way for tourists, were not appearing until the 1880's. Although a visitor seemed unlikely there were probably very few people in Polperro itself who had the time, knowledge or money to take up the complicated *New Art* in the early 1850's. One of the first things that strikes one about these photographs is that they are not commercial, which is not surprising perhaps since the fishing community of Polperro would have been a poor market. This photographer obviously fits into the category of gifted amateur, and most probably like his contemporaries — writers such as Lewis Carroll (active 1856-1880) and Emile Zola, or painters like Degas and Vuillard, photography was secondary to a main interest. He was a 'first generation amateur' as opposed to a 'second generation professional', men like Frank Sutcliffe, who was one of the first to devote his whole life to photography.

The Polperro portraits may not be as good as Carroll's, nor the genre pictures as good as Hill and Adamson's. However, the work reveals the life of one small area taken over a period of 25 years at a very early date and this makes it fairly unique. The portraits are simple and lack romantic backdrops and clutter of ornament then in vogue, and the outdoor group scenes are superbly arranged, often involving a lot of figures posed in depth. The photographer followed, or perhaps foresaw, the advice Lake Price gave in 1858 for those attempting marine subjects 'ashore'. 'It is quite within the scope and province of such a photographic subject that groups of analogous figures, which are always at hand, should be introduced; observing only the caution given in another place, and make the picture if possible, tell a story, or at least let its figures have their occupation and attentions within it, and not directed to the camera.'

Sutcliffe had said 'It took a clever man to be a photographer. He had to be an artist, a chemist and a mechanical engineer all rolled into one. He also had to be even tempered and resourceful!' For more than a year the identity of this *Hamlet Leonardo* was to remain a mystery.

The photographer would almost certainly have remained anonymous had not Dr. Turk mentioned that there was in existence a diary of observations on the life of a rookery written by a patient of Jonathan Couch's in the mid-1840's, which he had not seen but which seemed of great interest.

The first clues came on the first page, for by way of intro-
duction, Jonathan had written the following in 1850:

'The history of this volume is . . . that a Gentleman had returned
from a distant climate to Trelawne, in a very imperfect state of
health; in which it became necessary to prescribe for him a sort
and degree of occupation which should lay him under the
necessity of constant attention, without inconvenience or anxiety.
He was requested to observe the actions and habits of the Rooks
through the varying months of the year; and the volume which
follows is the result.'

Opposite this Thomas had added the following in 1870:

'The Gentleman thus set to work by my Father to chronicle the
life of a Rookery was Mr. Lewis Harding, a nephew of Sir Harry
Trelawny, Bart; of Trelawne, in Pelynt. He was a great invalid, and
resided at Trelawne for many years, from whence he moved to
Polperro.'

Here at last was a man who had the education, financial status
and patience to take up the *New Art*. Furthermore he would
have been a good friend of Jonathan's, hence the numerous
portraits, and yet a contemporary of Thomas, hence the pictures
taken after the former's death.

In Thomas' own printed copy of *The History of Polperro*, which
is interleaved with blank pages for the addition of further notes,

Thomas had pasted in a copy of one of the photographs of fishermen which also appears in the fully illustrated handwritten version. Beneath this picture he had written 'Polperro fishermen in fishing costume (Mr. Harding).' This was the only reference to the photographer we were ever to find. The reply to a letter to Douglas Puckey confirmed that Harding was the name he had been unable to remember. A successful search for his will revealed that he was a photographer, a Catholic and a bachelor. The diary, written when he was 41, shows he was well educated and spoke French. From the improvement of his handwriting in the diary it is clear that the unusual nature of Couch's treatment had the desired effect. If, as Dr. Turk suggests, Harding was suffering from a nervous disorder, it is interesting to compare the remedy more commonly employed at that date with that prescribed by Jonathan Couch and so recognise Couch's advanced thinking. In his book about Victorian cruelty *Night's Black Angels* Ronald Pearsall writes: 'Many people suffering from stress or what we would now describe as anxiety neurosis were decoyed into asylums by rapacious friends. They were told that they would be going for a few weeks into a rest home, only to find that once the committal order had been signed there was no way back to the outside world. Not surprisingly, many of these people were driven mad by the conditions prevailing in the asylums . . . Not all the men and women who signed committal papers for their spouses or relatives were evil; some thought it was for the best, and put their reliance on the doctor. When he told them that they should not visit the patient as it would agitate him or her and worsen the affliction they obediently agreed. Occasionally they got to hear of the actual conditions.'

But the diary not only demonstrates Couch's ability to choose an effective cure, it is also ahead of its time as a natural history study. In his book *The Leaping Hare* (1972), G.E. Evans mentions the lack of work done on particular animals or birds until only recently: 'But this is perhaps understandable. People like Gilbert White were rare, and until this century, in any case, most naturalists were wide-ranging in their observations, seldom concentrating on one particular bird or creature. Moreover it probably needs someone with a scientific training, someone with the necessary objectivity, attention to detail, a single-minded persistence, and — most of all — the time to carry through the exacting task of concentrating on one animal.'

Harding's diary is a notable exception as is the work of the poet William Cowper who was a manic-depressive. Cowper made valuable observations of hares, which he kept as pets for about twelve years, and though this was nothing like as intensive a study as Harding's, it is thought to have helped him. It is just possible Couch had the idea of using the study of rooks as 'occupational therapy' from reading Cowper's account of his hares written in 1784 and published in *The Gentleman's Magazine*. In this account Cowper makes the following comments: 'In the year 1774, being much indisposed both in mind and body, incapable of diverting myself either with company or books, and yet in a condition that made some diversion necessary, I was glad of anything that would engage my attention, without fatiguing it . . . perceiving that, in the management of such an animal, and in the attempt to tame it, I should find just that sort of employment which my case required.'

There is one other reference to Harding and that is in Bertha Couch's *Life of Jonathan Couch* in which she mentions a Mr.

Harding sending Jonathan two cases of valuable Australian butter-
flies while he was abroad. This might have been Lewis's father,
John Cooke Harding, but if it was Lewis, then Australia could
have been the 'distant climate' where he became so ill.

A letter to nearby Sclerder Abbey where Harding was buried,
revealed that Lewis had taught in a Roman Catholic Seminary in
Sydney, having gone out with Bishop Polding in 1835. According
to the archives of the Bishop of Sydney, Harding was stationed at
the penal settlement of Norfolk Island between 1840 and 1845
and had returned to England arriving at Trelawne in 1846. There
was no record of ill-health.

We know hardly anything of Lewis Harding. Perhaps like
William Loughrin, the local coastguard Couch trained to prepare
fish, he is one of the latter's disciples whose work has far outlived
any memory of the man.

To summarise, where Couch wrote 'a Gentleman had returned
from a distant climate in a very imperfect state of health', we now
know that in 1846 Harding (1806-1893), the nephew of Sir Harry
Trelawny, returned after an absence of eleven years in Australia.
The illness he suffered from was most probably a serious nervous
disorder, the novel course of treatment suggested was successful
and the resulting diary an interesting document in the development of natural history. Some years after he was cured and
probably before he moved to Polperro, Harding took up photography, perhaps even as added therapy. Trelawne had a number of
tenant farmers and Harding refers to some of them in the diary. It
is probably these he portrays in the two early farming scenes
owned by Douglas Puckey. After his move to Polperro he seems to
have confined himself to the village for there is no mention of him
in any of Cornwall's learned societies or as a part-time teacher in

'...a Gentleman had returned from a distant climate to
Trelawne, in a very imperfect state of health.'

any nearby school. All the photographs that survive, apart from the farming scenes, two views of Trelawne and one other, are of Polperro.

Without Harding's portraits we would have no likeness of Richard and only a painting of Jonathan. His series of eighty-two straightforward head and shoulder portraits of fishermen taken in the 1860's, alone assures him a place in the histories of photography and sociology. But it is the combined strength of his photographs and Couch's *History of Polperro* that give us such a vivid picture of a time and place.

Two views of Trelawne by Harding

Two miles from Polperro lies Trelawne, an ancient house dating back to before the Conquest. For hundreds of years it was owned by the equally ancient Trelawny family who originally lived at Trelawny in Altarnun. It was probably the similarity of the name that led the Elizabethan Jonathan to purchase Trelawne in Pelynt. During the early 19th century it was owned by Harding's uncle Sir Harry, whose daughter, Ann Laetitia, became head of the house when the latter departed to spend his last days in Italy.

Two people who visited the house during Harding's lifetime were Edward John Trelawny, the friend of Byron and Shelley, and in 1833 the Victorian novelist Eliza Bray. She was collecting material for a romantic novel based on the love letters between Sir Harry and his first cousin, Laetitia, written before the latter's father finally gave his consent to the marriage. Mrs. Bray went from Trelawne to Polperro, which she thought even more beautiful than Looe.

'The descent to it is so steep, that I, who was not accustomed to the path, could only get down by clinging to Mr. Bray's arm for support; it was slippery, and so rocky, that in some places there were some steps cut in the road for the convenience of the passenger. The view of the little port, the old town in the bottom (if town it can be called), the cliffs and the spike rocks, that start up in the wildest and most abrupt manner, breaking the direct sweep of the waves towards the harbour, altogether produced such a combination of magnificent coast scenery as may truly be called sublime . . . We called on the medical gentleman (Dr. Jonathan Couch), before noticed in these pages, who resided at a small dwelling in Polperro. We found him surrounded by his books and curiosities . . .'

Sir Harry Trelawny became a Methodist soon after 1776 and then a Calvinist, later he took Holy Orders in the Church of England and finally died at Laverno in Italy, having become a Roman Catholic Bishop.

'A good monograph of the rook could not fail to be as interesting as its compilation would be laborious.' William Yarrell c. 1844.

Harding would have produced neither diary nor photographs had it not been for Jonathan Couch. It is therefore interesting to note what lay behind the doctor's unusual choice of treatment. Three men to whose work this choice was related were Charles Darwin, Gilbert White and William Yarrell.

Darwin had said 'After reading Gilbert White's *The Natural History of Selborne* I studied the habits of birds and wondered why every gentleman did not become an ornithologist.' This was probably a little how Couch had felt, for having given up the chance of a successful career as a London surgeon he returned to Polperro to become a poorly paid local doctor in order to pursue his natural history studies. Although Couch never had any cause to regret his decision, Darwin seemed to. The implications of his evolutionary discoveries frightened him so much that he instructed his wife to publish the paper only after his death and turned his attention to barnacles. As Wallace wrote 'The one great result which I claim for my paper of 1858 is that it compelled Darwin to write and publish his Origin of Species without further delay.' The delay having been fifteen years.

Gilbert White

In 1768 Gilbert White wrote 'If fortune had settled me near the seaside, or near some great river, my natural propensity would soon have urged me to have made myself acquainted with their productions: but as I have lived mostly in inland parts, and in an upland district, my knowledge of fishes extends little farther than to those common sorts which our brooks and lakes produce.' Thus Couch became a kind of seaside Gilbert White.

The naturalist William Yarrell was a friend of Couch's and visited by the latter on his infrequent trips to London. In 1885 Leonard Blomefield wrote of Yarrell 'In the hope of getting something new or rare for his 'Birds' or 'Fishes' he closely examined the poulterers' and fishmongers' shops when walking in the streets, and his sharp eye would immediately detect anything exposed for sale he was not familiar with, when he would stop and make enquiries. I have been with him when he would stand and handle the fish on the board looking closely into their characters.' One of the chief differences between the two naturalists was that whereas Yarrell obtained his fish from Billingsgate, Couch received his straight from the net. Furthermore, since Couch had made a device which sprinkled water over fish as he painted them, he was able to portray specimens in their true colours and not the drab hues seen on the fishmongers' slab. Blomefield wrote of an occasion on which Yarrell rectified this imbalance with Couch. 'One summer, I think it must have been 1831, Yarrell and myself, being full of the subject of the British Fishes, agreed upon a trip to the south coast.' However, during excursions out in local fishing boats, both were too seasick to continue.

William Yarrell

At the time of Harding's illness Couch had just completed his book on instinct in animals and from this it is clear he already had more than a passing interest in rooks. That Harding was educated and lived in the middle of a large rookery provided Couch with an opportunity of which he took full advantage.

Dr. Frank Turk, whose awareness of the existence of the rookery diary led to the identity of the photographer, has made the following comments on it:

In 1847 Harding was, in a small way, to make history; he did

Jonathan Couch

'He was requested to observe the actions and habits of the rooks through the varying months of the year.'

not attempt to do so, he was unaware of doing so and indeed, until a year or so ago, no-one else knew that he had done so. The manner of his minor brush with history was thus:

There is, among the family papers of Miss Foy Quiller-Couch of Lanhydrock, a bound volume of manuscript notes in what, as we now know, is Lewis Harding's handwriting. It is entitled 'Life in a Rookery — collected for Jonathan Couch'. Divided into twelve parts, each corresponding to one of the twelve months of the year, the first page is titled as follows — Rooks/and/ Rookery/for/September 1847 — Journal of daily occurrences/and Summary/for the Month/of September. So little could the author have valued his notes as a serious contribution to Natural History that nowhere in the manuscript has he recorded his name or given a clue as to his identity. Were it not for the two almost fortuitous introductory notes inserted at the front of the manuscript, the first by Jonathan and the second by Thomas, we may forever have been ignorant of who the author was and the circumstances that brought the work into being.

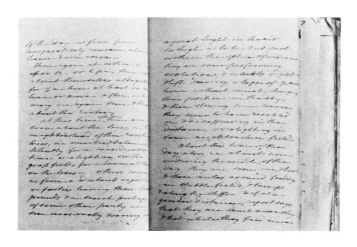

Despite these explicit notes, the journal — the existence of which has been known in certain quarters for a long time but more as a semi-legendary work than as a surviving document — has sometimes been referred to among interested scholars as 'Couch's Rook Manuscript'. The near anonymity with which Harding surrounded himself for the 87 years of his life almost covered him once again in connection with his journal.

But history was being made here in more ways than are immediately apparent. It is arguable that this is one of the earliest recorded instances of successful occupational therapy practised in Britain. There is reason to think, on several grounds, that Lewis Harding suffered from some nervous disorder and it is worth noting that Phillipe Pinel's book *Traité medico-philosophique sur l'alienation mentale* — the first to advocate occupational therapy for such cases — was published in 1801. An English translation by D.D. Davis (*Treatise on Insanity*) appeared in 1806 and this may well have been in Couch's library. Indeed the idea of setting Harding this particular task may equally well have come from this source because, in the section 'General Plan of the Work', mention is made of the fact that 'Nothing has more contributed to the rapid improvement of modern natural history, than the spirit of minute and accurate observation that has distinguished its votaries'. Again in the section dealing with 'Laborious occupations recommended for convalescents', Pinel instances a case of a riotous maniac for whom he prescribed 'employment of a rural nature, such as I knew would meet his taste' and records that 'From that time I never observed any confusion nor extravagance in his ideas'. It is possible that such a description of the outcome might have applied closely to Harding.

But Lewis Harding was to make history more certainly in quite another way. He was probably the first naturalist to make *daily* observations, often for many hours each day, on one species of animal for a whole year. More than a hundred years before, Abraham Trembley had published (1744) his detailed observations of *Hydra* but these were neither chronologically successive nor were they systematic. Gilbert White's were certainly sometimes systematic but seldom so over prolonged periods. This is indeed the importance of Harding's work. That Couch should have set his patient to this subject as a regime of recording is, undoubtedly, connected with the fact that in this same year (1847) Couch had published his *Illustrations of Instinct deducted from the Habits of British Animals*. The treatment here is largely anecdotal as was then the custom; significantly too the Rook has considerable mention in the book. Couch's mind may well have been still taken up with the behaviour of this species and perhaps he had already seen the necessity of prolonged and successive observations of it when he recommended the task to Harding.

The matters to which Harding most commonly gives his attention are the movements of birds at different times of the day, seasons of the year and states of the weather. He notes the fact that, as in Gilbert White's time, they mate on the ground — an action that the present day 'Rook society' seems to find unfashionable. He deals a little with the moult, but does not deal with the curious loss of the face feathers* nor, in any detail, with the nature of the food; indeed detailed knowledge of this last was not to be provided until the work of Holbrung in Germany in 1906.

Harding was, in fact, an amateur naturalist and one typical of his time. He had sent back natural history collections, the fruits of his sojourn in Australia, to both Couch and the museum of the Royal Institution of Cornwall. Under Couch's tutelage he became more scientific and detached — so much so that, at the end of the journal we find entries that give evidence of almost professional concern for exactitude.

It might well be too that these daily labours in the field were a strongly formative influence in providing him with the 'photographic eye' of which, in later years, he was to give such abundant evidence.

*This question of the face feathers caused a good deal of controversy among naturalists. Most were of the opinion that they were worn off — 'by often thrusting the Bill into the ground, to fetch out Earthworms so that the flesh thereabouts is bare, and appears of a whitish colour' as Francis Willughby put it in 1678.

In 1838 Charles Waterton, the eccentric naturalist and traveller, wrote 'Bewick is the only one in Professor Rennie's long and fanciful list of rudimentary naturalists, literary naturalists and philosophic naturalists, and original observers, who give us anything satisfactory concerning this nudity'.

Waterton was a practical man and rather than enter the debate with so much hot air he reared two young rooks in a cage and discovered that the face feathers actually fell off naturally. But Waterton's flamboyance made him enemies. 'Waterton has hitherto published nothing, respecting the economy or faculties of animals, of the least use to natural history', wrote Professor Rennie. 'This being the case', replied Waterton, 'I am trying to make up my deficiency in pen and ink, by establishing a sylvan enclosure, which any ornithologist is allowed to enter; and where he will have an opportunity of correcting, by actual observation, some of those errors which appear in the second edition of Montagu, by James Rennie, A.M. A.L.S. Moreover, sometimes, in a jocose kind of way, I tell them I like to have all kinds of birds around me; and that I cannot find in my heart to kill a poor jay for sucking an egg when I know

'That I myself, carniverous sinner,
Had pullets yesterday for dinner.'

After he was cured Harding probably divided his time between Trelawne and Polperro.

It was perhaps in the 1850's that Harding moved to live in his father's cottage at Polperro. We do not know however if this move was followed by an involvement with photography, or if an interest in the *New Art* had begun while he was still at Trelawne. Harding worked with the collodion wet-plate process (1851-c.1880), so we have a clear picture of the large amount of equipment he needed from the start. Because the ether in the collodion evaporated quickly it was necessary to develop the plate directly after exposure and this meant one needed a mobile darkroom. Although these farming scenes were taken with a small camera, the equipment required to develop a single glass plate could still weigh a hundred pounds. Since these pictures and the two of Trelawne are almost the only ones not of Polperro, the weight of the equipment and the steepness of the hills may have confined Harding thereafter to Polperro. It was the lot of the wet-plate photographer to become increasingly parochial: as he grew more accomplished he would obtain larger cameras, consequently suffering greater immobility, which increased as he grew older.

 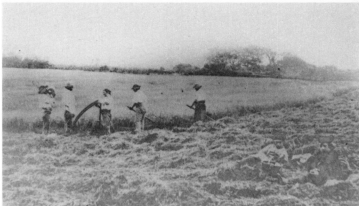

These two farming pictures would have required an exposure of a few seconds and Frank Sutcliffe, the Whitby photographer, had something to say about the difficulties involved with recording such scenes.

'Perhaps the most attractive subject in the hayfield was the mowing of it, as it was the most musical. The regular swish of the three scythes, as the mowers went forward in unison, was a note to be remembered. But this was a subject which taxed the speed of the early dry-plate to the utmost, and the wise photographer kept back his plates and exposed them when a mower stood up to whet his lye, or in other words to sharpen his scythe. If it were not possible to get pictures of arrested motion, it was possible to ask the mower to 'Keep still just as you are' when a happy position was noticed. Here again music, as different from noise, was heard when the scythe was being whetted. Then in those days all the farmer's sons and daughters, women and girls turned out to turn the hay, with forks and hay rakes. Each photograph was carefully set up, and the right moment waited for. He would then ask the figures to keep still for a few seconds while they were being photographed. In many cases this meant that the figure would put down his or her work and stand at attention, looking at the lens — 'Now keep still, please, just as you are, without looking up.'

Harding obviously shared Lake Price's viewpoint, for in 1858 the latter wrote: 'What is most requisite is that the figures composing such groups should have an air of natural occupation, as if in their usual vocations or amusements.'

'The use of oxen for draught is fast going out; but it was a common thing a few years since to see two or even three yoke dragging lazily the plough through the furrow, while the plough-boy drove them with a goad, or encouraged them with a measured chant, (the sweetest of our rural sounds), in which the names of the oxen, 'Spark and Beauty, Brisk and Lively, Good-luck and Speedwell' might be distinguished. Now oxen are reared only for the market and it is more common to see the ploughman holding his plough, drawn by a pair of horses, which he directs himself by two reins, dispensing with the plough-boy and his goad.' *History of Polperro* J. Couch.

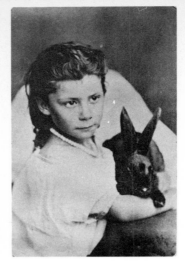

There are no pictures of rooks by Harding and it is most unlikely he ever took any. This is because photographing wildlife was not really possible until the late 1880's or 1890's. In the primeval days of the calotype, probably even slow moving pets lived in constant dread of the prolonged affection their masters might suddenly unleash on them. The dog in this calotype by Llewelyn for example was held fast for several minutes, and even the rabbit in Harding's later wet-plate portrait probably had to be caught between twitches. Apart from such occasional uses of an animal as a prop, wild life was at first mostly confined to an almost forgotten behind-the-scenes role.

During the arduous moments of sitting before a camera in the early days, when cameras liked to take their time, a bird in a cage was sometimes employed to keep the sitter's eyes in one position, and the expression in them alive. Perhaps the size of the cage was related to the focal length of the lens, so that any movement of the bird would not cause too noticeable a movement of the eyes rivetted upon it. Failure to observe this might have resulted in a face fascinated into immobility, but with frenzied whirls either side of the nose.

When plates grew more sensitive and sitting for a portrait no longer entailed being screwed to the floor, bird cages began to appear beside the sitter. However, it was still some time before the bird, rather than the cage, became the subject, and it was not really until the late 1880's that the camera ceased to be confused by the unpredictable toing and froing of fauna.

At first the problem of photographing wild life was solved with the aid of stuffed specimens like this deer, doomed to an existence of eternal alertness, or the otter, its base contrived into the riverbank by Llewelyn for a twenty minute exposure in 1856. But there is a link between photography and taxidermy as intricate as that between butterfly and caterpillar, (John Cooper of St. Ives for example, was a taxidermist who turned into a photographer) and when in the early 1890's the famous Kearton brothers opened everyone's eyes to the possibilities of photographing wild life from hides, they did not put the taxidermist out of business, but rather did the opposite.

How this occurred is explained by Richard Kearton in a passage from one of his many books about how he and Cherry successfully photographed a wood pigeon. 'As the Greeks of old entered Troy inside a wooden horse, I thought that we might, by the employment of a similar kind of stealth, perhaps penetrate some of the secrets of the bird world, so induced our old friend Mr. Rowland Ward, to stuff us an ox, complete in every detail. He gave the animal such lifelike bovine calm and stolidity as readily to deceive members of the 'genus homo' at the distance of a few paces. This was distinctly encouraging, so we fixed our dummy bullock up close beside a skylark's nest containing young ones. The parent bird came home directly with food, and without a moment's hesitation or questioning alighted and gave it to her offspring under the very muzzle of the doubly inoffensive ox. Having figured the unsuspecting skylark and her young to our satisfaction, we next removed the deception to the edge of a secluded pond, where cattle were in the habit of coming to quench their thirst, and birds to drink and bathe. One blazing hot July day, as I crouched in the internal regions of the stuffed ox, with the lens of my camera (minus the tripod) peeping through a round hole in the hide of the beast in front of me, I heard a Ring Dove commence to coo lazily in an oak tree close by, presently down it came and began to drink in the most confidential manner. Instead of taking a sip, raising its head and allowing the liquid to trickle down its throat, it thrust the bill deep into the pool and commenced to suck the water up like a horse, reminding me of a statement made by Gilbert White in his immortal Natural History of Selborne to this effect. As she drank, she sent ever swelling-rings forth on the bosom of the sequestered pool, and the camera has recorded their appearance with wonderful fidelity in our plate.'

But the Keartons did not stop at oxen.

'Although splendidly deceptive, our stuffed ox was an expensive hiding contrivance, intolerably back aching at all times, and particularly stuffy during hot weather, and, I fear, not to be recommended without certain reservations to the budding naturalist photographer. After trying our dummy ox with success upon a variety of species in the South of England, it one day occurred to me that a sheep, similarly prepared, from which to photograph birds on moor and mountain, might prove useful. I therefore had one stuffed in a lying down position, with a hollow body for the reception of the camera, minus the tripod, and with a hole in the chest for the lens to look through. Meadow Pipits, Wheatear, and Sandpipers were deceived by it, although the sudden discovery of the huge black eye staring straight at her from the breast of the sheep scared the last-named bird rather badly at first.'

That same wild life which had begun caged behind the camera and then chirruped its way into the picture, had finally run amuck, engulfing the photographer together with all his equipment. Was it genius or madness that caused the photographer, faced with a lifeless ox propped up in a sunny glade and smelling of mothballs, to turn himself around and climb inside it?

With the aid of artificial trees, fake rubbish heaps and hollow rocks, the Keartons turned voyeur and infiltrated the scenery so as to record the private lives of the timidest of creatures. Richard was determined that 'Stuffed specimens should be set up from photographs taken from wild life, and not photographs taken from stuffed specimens.'

Others employed equally devious tactics. One writer suggested constructing a dummy camera out of an old tin, painting stripes for bellows, adding a cork lens and mounting the whole affair on some sticks. When the bird, whose nest this was placed near, had grown accustomed to the intruder, it was replaced by the real thing and controlled from a safe distance with a long pneumatic tube.

Another writer insisted 'Nothing is quite so good as the gradual approach of the camera in position in the tent.' However, this sort of grandmother's footsteps was not a success with birds who were inclined to nest on ledges above the ocean, and descending on a rope laden with camera and plates was a far cry from being gently asphyxiated inside an ox.

It was probably at Osprey Cottage in Polperro that Harding took most of the portraits of the fishermen and their families. There are a number of views of the harbour taken from his garden, including some exposed during a storm.

Polperro suffered particularly badly from storms, as Couch relates:

'We suffer greatly from south-westerly gales, but the winds which affect us most are those blowing from points between south and east. We have records of gales from the latter direction, some of which have been already mentioned, which have threatened to demolish the town. In the time of a storm Polperro is a striking scene of bustle and excitement. The noise of the wind as it roars up the coomb, the hoarse rumbling of the angry sea, the shouts of the fishermen engaged in securing their boats, and the screams of the women and children, carrying the tidings of the latest disaster, are a peculiarly melancholy assemblage of sounds, especially when heard at midnight. All who can render assistance are out of their beds, helping the sailors and fishermen; lifting the boats out of reach of the sea, or taking the furniture of the ground floors to a place of safety. The excitement is extreme, but not more than is necessary to the occasion, for with the loss of his boat the fisherman is deprived of the most important of his possessions, as well as of his means of obtaining a livelihood. When the first streak of morning light comes, bringing no cessation of the storm, but only serving to show the devastation it has made, the effect is still more dismal. The wild fury of the waves is a sight of no mean grandeur as it dashes over the peak, and falls on its jagged summit, from whence it streams down its sides in a thousand waterfalls, and foams at its base. The infuriated sea sweeps over the piers, and striking against the rocks and houses on the warren side, rebounds towards the strand, and washes fragments of houses and boats into the streets where the receding tide leaves them strewn in sad confusion. Storms of this kind I have seen several times, though happily they are not of very frequent occurrence.'

'On the 20th January, 1817, a storm of unusual violence occurred. Its direction was from the south east, a very unfavourable point; and the sea, being driven by a furious gale to an extraordinary height, swept away a great deal of property. It covered the 'Green' from one end to the other, and reached to the top of the parapet wall of the bridge there, a height of five feet, and stopped the mill-wheel with its violence. The tide, in a body, swept over the highest point of the Peak, and, as near as the eye could judge, at double the height of the rock, not in mere spray, but in a solid body of water. The premises occupied by the Coastguard were soon levelled with the beach; the shipwright's yard on Consona rocks, and a cellar and chamber over it, were demolished, with two *stop* and two *tuck* seans there stored. About thirty large boats and a great many smaller were utterly destroyed, so that scarcely a piece could be recognised, the wreck strewing the harbour and the streets. Happily no lives were lost, though the danger to many was imminent. The damage done was estimated at upwards of £2,000.'

The 'Duke of Cornwall' pier, on the left of this picture, greatly improved the safety of the harbour. Jonathan Couch, who was chairman of the committee, had conceived and drawn up the plans for it, as well as going to London and convincing the Government of its need. The foundation stone was laid by W.D. Boase, Inspector of Charities, on 5th September, 1861 'amid much rejoicing'.

Jonathan Couch (1789-1870) was one of the most eminent and widely known Cornishmen of his generation. He was the only child of elderly Polperro parents, who rather than expose him to the dangers of a seafaring life had concentrated on his education. From the local Dame School he went to nearby Trelawne Manor, where he was taught by a Jesuit priest. Later he went to Bodmin grammar school and from there he was apprenticed to John Rice, a physician in Looe. Finally, after attending Medical School at Guy's and St. Thomas's in London, he returned to settle in Polperro with his wife, where in spite of hardships and poverty, he chose to spend the rest of his life. Tragically his wife, Jane Rundle, died after one year. Five years later he married Jane Quiller and they had six children, of whom Richard, Thomas, John and Jonathan all became doctors. When she died, he, now 69, married a girl of 22, Sarah Roose, and they had three daughters.

Couch's interests and abilities were varied and numerous, and a list of his published papers seems endless. As Thomas wrote:

'At the age of 14 he watched and recorded the actions of a bee, which built a hole in his father's door-post; and his observation on physical phenomena were continued, in unbroken series, until within a few days of his death . . . Jonathan Couch was evidently a born naturalist. Set down, in a remote nook, without guidance or aid, a path seems to have been struck out for him, which he perseveringly and successfully followed.'

Couch, who in the photograph below is seen standing outside his own house surrounded by his neighbours, could say 'I have this day 5th September, 1861, attended the birth of a child, who is the latest of six generations I have known intimately, both on the father's and mother's side; four of these I have attended in child-birth.'

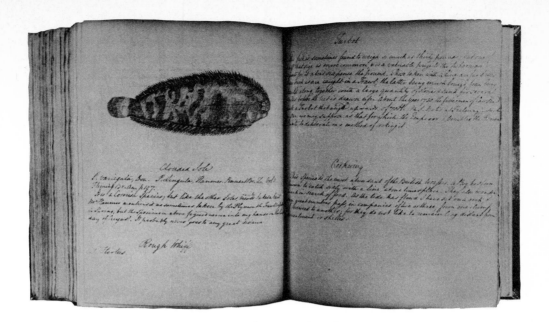

Jonathan Couch's major work *History of the Fishes of the British Islands* was the fruit of sixty years work and owes much to the local fishermen who helped him by bringing ashore any uncommon fish they caught in their nets. As Bertha Couch relates in her *Life of Jonathan Couch*:

'A picture well known to Polperro people, would be the Doctor seated on a fish maund busily engaged with a pencil or paint brush in transferring to paper the correct dimensions or beautiful colours of some strange fish. Listening the while to the quaintly expressed account of its capture, or what they may have noticed of its peculiarities.'

In 1865 Couch himself wrote an account for 'Fishing Gossip' entitled 'A Torpedo at one end of the line', which was about a particular specimen that proved more difficult than most to capture.

'On the south coast of Cornwall ten men proceeded together on a fishing expedition, and were successful in getting a good quantity of fish into their net, and which, while the bunt of the net remained in the water, they prepared to take with their hands into the boat. But while thus engaged, the man employed in handling the fish was heard to utter what his comrade described as a most unearthly yell, and then he fell backwards to the bottom of the boat, so that his associate supposed that he had been at the least seized with sudden illness. Several minutes passed before he was able to utter a word, and consequently to relieve the anxiety of his friends how it was he had been smitten; but one of his companions, who manifested less sympathy with the terror under which he laboured than the rest, ascribed it to being what he termed nervous; but as in answer to this the sufferer ascribed what he had felt to something contained in the net, this individual exclaimed that if the devil were there he would fetch him out, and then, turning upward his shirt-sleeves, he proceeded to grasp in good earnest the fish that were in the purse. But this formidable ray was a match for all this bluster, and presently this man uttered a yell to the full as loud as the scream of his comrade, on hearing which all was consternation on board the boat. The cause evidently was a fish, but of what sort no-one seemed to imagine. It was clear that something must be done, and by some means yet untried; and after some consideration, one of the company procured a pole, and with it made a thrust at the fish, in the supposition that at a safe distance he might do so with impunity. In this, however, he found himself mistaken; and, as in the instance of the case mentioned by the Greek poet Oppian, where the shock passed through the line, a shock was sent through his limbs and, like his comrades, he fell down to the bottom of the boat. Fortunately it happened that among these fishermen there was one who possessed some knowledge of the nature of a fish able to exert powers which might produce the effects witnessed, and all the crew were resolute in their determination not to be overcome. Various then were the contrivances they were prepared to adopt to get their formidable assailant on board; and yet it so happened that before they succeeded every one of them was made to experience the powers of their antagonist. It may be supposed that after so many discharges of the torporific or galvanic influence, the powers of this fish had become exhausted, but their experience had taught them not to trust in this, and therefore a quantity of seaweed was procured on which the bag or purse was laid, with the fish still remaining in it, and in this way the whole was brought to land.'

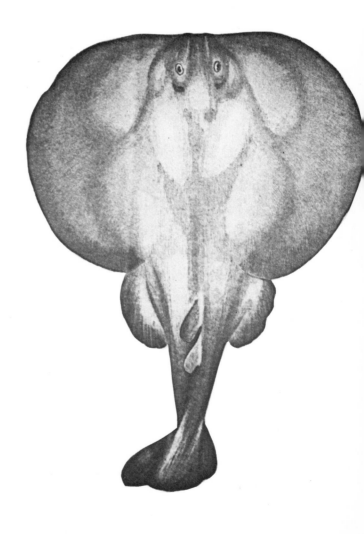

'Near the strand on the Lansallos side are the 'fish-scales', or market, where you may often see a busy group of fishermen, clad in Guernsey-frocks, sou'westers, and sea-boots, bargaining, by a sort of auction, with loquacious jowters, i.e., travelling fishmongers, for the contents of the 'ocean-smelling osier' (too sweet a term, perhaps, for the brown slimy pannier); or for piles of cod, ling, and conger, too bulky to be so contained.' *History of Polperro*.

'... and with such plentie therof hath God stuffed the bowels of this little Angle, that (as Aftiages dreamed of his daughter) it overfloweth England, watereth Christendom, and is derived to a great part of the world besides.' *Richard Carew, Survey of Cornwall, 1602.*

While Jonathan's interests lay in the depths of the ocean, Richard's for some years lay underground. In the mid-19th century, Cornish mining was booming and when Richard moved from Polperro, where there were no mines, to become a surgeon in the Penzance St. Just district, where there were many, he could not help noticing the difference in life expectancy between fishermen and miners. Both professions had their natural hazards, but while there were plenty of old fishermen, for a miner to reach fifty was uncommon. Disease worked from within as successfully as they worked in their deep lairs, and Richard made a study of the mortality rate, publishing the results in a series of papers between 1857 and 1860.

In 1859 a Mr. John Roberton wrote a paper entitled 'The insalubrity of the deep Cornish mines and as a consequence the physical degeneracy and the early deaths of the mining population.' In this he mentions meeting Mr. Couch — 'Surgeon to several mines. distinguished naturalist, and well known for the investigation he has made ...   Most of the inhabitants of St. Just', writes Mr. Couch, 'except those who have no connection with mining operations, have a bloodless and unhealthy look. I have weighed' says Mr. Couch '1,100 men and find they lose 3¾ pounds, on the average, during the time they are underground, some as much as ten pounds.'

If Richard's interests lay underground for a while, they were by no means confined there, for although he only lived about half as long as his father, he turned his attention to almost as great a variety of subjects. He made considerable contributions to the knowledge of Cornish fossils, fish and crustacea, as well as writing a number of papers, particularly on Geology and Zoology.

The greatest exponent of Cornish underground photography was the appropriately named John Burrow. One of the subjects that interested him was the way in which miners were lowered to their work. In Carew's day 'the workmen are let down and taken up in a stirrup, by two men who wind the rope.' They also used ladders a good deal. In Richard's time, although the mines were deeper, they were better ventilated. But there was still the gruelling task of getting to the surface after a hard day's work. In 1864 a commission headed by Lord Kinnaird reported that there were mines at which not less than three hours were expended by the miner in going to and from his work. Even in 1892, when Burrow was photographing, conditions were hardly better. Because he used several magnesium lamps (of his own design) to light a scene, this picture of the Dolcoath man-engine not only does not show this man-engine in its true light, which was usually a single candle flaring precariously on the head of a travelling miner, but it was not typical of the hundreds of other Cornish mines that did not have one at all. Cages were used and whims and of course the ladders that sapped any of the miner's remaining strength and left him sweating as he surfaced into the cold air. Burrow's photographs showed the world for the first time a little of what it was like.

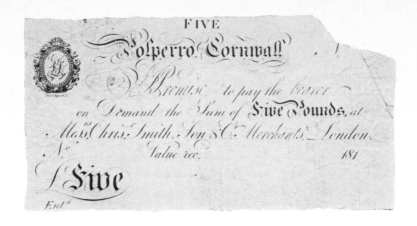

Although Polperro was at times the poorest of places, occasionally its fortunes were dramatically reversed. Privateering — the capturing of enemy ships by privately owned but licensed vessels — brought in huge sums of money. In 1793 the 'Brilliant', captained by John Quiller, captured the 'Santa Balanez', a Spanish ship for which the prize money received was £8,800. As was usual this was divided up among the shareholders, who were mostly Quillers — the great seafaring family that Jonathan Couch married into. One of the shareholders in the 'Santa Balanez' success was Zephaniah Job (1752-1822), a man born in St. Agnes and educated as a mine captain, who fled to Polperro for refuge after a fight. There he made a living as a school teacher and then as a banker, eventually becoming, apart from Couch, the single greatest benefactor to Polperro.

Without Job's few surviving account books of ships fitted out as privateers between 1777 and 1815 it would be hard to believe the large sums of money involved in both privateering and smuggling at Polperro. For example between 1778 and 1800 Job transferred to Guernsey the sum of £131,363 to pay wine merchants for goods bought by his Polperro smuggling clients for whom he acted as financial agent. Not only was this merely the wholesale price but Job did not deal with all the smugglers in Polperro. As well as looking after the accounts of privateers and smugglers he became Steward, business manager and banker to Sir Harry and Lady Trelawny. In 1796 he arranged a loan from John Quiller to Sir Harry of £1,300 and later in 1812 was himself owed as much as £4,000 by Sir Harry. He also issued his own banknotes, took charge of the pilchard export trade to Italy, was a corn trader, seed merchant, coal importer, timber merchant, importer of linen, and carried out conveyancing and arranged life assurance policies. As with Couch the list of his abilities and accomplishments is endless.

The smugglers and Polperro owed a lot to Job, it was thanks to his good management and guidance that men like John Quiller spent more on the education of one daughter than the Rector of Lansallos spent on two. As Sheila de Burlet notes 'Any loss to the Exchequer of the day through smuggling was fully repaid by the capture of enemy ships, and indeed the sons and grandsons of many Polperro families like the Couchs, Quillers, Rowetts and Rendles have made a contribution to British life and learning in scientific and medical knowledge that by any standard can be called impressive. . . . Job died at Kellow on 31st January, 1822 and was attended in his last illness by Dr. Jonathan Couch (then aged 33) whose account came to £12 13s 6d.'

Robert Jeffrey is remembered rather for something that happened to him than for anything he did. Son of a Polperro publican he was impressed into the navy in 1807 at the age of 18 and left on an island in mid ocean for stealing rum. Unfortunately for Jeffrey 'Sombrero' was uninhabited and it was eight days before he was sighted and taken off by a passing ship. Meanwhile word had reached the Admiral of Captain Lake's barbarous deed and he was sent back to pick him up. But Jeffrey had by now recovered and was working as a blacksmith in America, little knowing the stir his disappearance was to cause back home. The House of Commons debated the cruelty of Lake's act and he was eventually court martialled, in spite of denying any knowledge that Sombrero was uninhabited and insisting it was covered in birds eggs.

After a thorough search Jeffrey was eventually found and brought back to England. The story had caught the public eye and pens flowed tears over his return to Polperro — although it seems he had never bothered to write to his mother, or had been too ashamed. A round of the London music halls as 'Jeffrey the Sailor' brought him enough money to purchase a trading schooner but in 1820 he died of tuberculosis, aged only 31.

William Rowett, born in 1806, captained ships to Australia and South America, later settling in Liverpool as a rope manufacturer. He wrote a pamphlet 'Sailing Directions for Approaching the Islands of Scilly', and suggested improvements in the design of an apparatus for lifting weights, invented 'The Cylinder Paddle Wheel' and in 1858 devised a system of protecting undersea telegraph cables, for which he obtained concessions from France for laying the cable between France and The United States.

John Quiller Rowett, born in 1876, became managing director of Rowett and Leakey, probably the world's largest shippers of rum, and made possible the Shackleton — Rowett expedition to the Antarctic with a donation of £70,000 in 1921.

The Scilly Isles. Anonymous photograph c.1890

Polperro harbour with William Rowett and family, c.1861

Hannah Hill Hitchens Rowett, b.1850

'The family is a disappointing one numerically, and resembles potatoes in having its best parts underground.' F.H. Perrycoste, 1903.

Frank H. Perrycoste

Sir Francis Galton

In 1903 Frank H. Perrycoste compiled a set of pedigrees of Polperro families for Sir Francis Galton, with fingerprints of nearly the whole population. As Perrycoste himself explained 'Sir Francis Galton asked me to collect the fingerprints as material for his study of the inheritance thereof . . . In order that these prints should be of any value it was necessary to show the relation of those fingerprinted to one another.' He had some difficulty in collecting the prints, for as Galton wrote in a letter to him dated 28th August, 1903:

'Your fault as a 'fingerprinter' is blottiness. This *cannot* occur if the ink be spread over the tin box with thinness. Whenever too much ink has been accidentally squeezed out, the superfluity would be removed by dabbing the over-inked rubber on waste paper.' But in the next letter, of 1st September, 1903, he congratulated Perrycoste.

'I have quite enough for provisional results, viz. 865 sets. Let me reiterate how strongly I feel my obligation to you. It is a grand collection that you have made for me . . . and I will do my best to do justice to the large material so laboriously obtained by you for me.'

Galton went on to sympathise with and encourage Perrycoste, though at the expense of the locals.

'I can assure you that I realise the difficulty in printing from the worn fingers of perhaps unwilling and often stupid fisherfolk. Small has sent me three full books taken during his holidays in North Cornwall. They are perfectly beautiful but they are taken from a non-labouring class.'

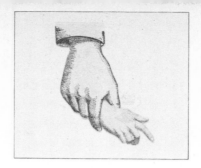

In an earlier letter he had suggested 'It is a good plan just before pressing the child's finger on the paper to direct its attention to the window, then its curled-up finger relaxes at once, and a good print is taken.'

Galton was soon confirmed in his belief that Polperro was a much inter-married group because of 'the much greater frequency of arches in their fingerprints, than occurs in the population at large.'

If Perrycoste had had problems obtaining fingerprints, it was nothing compared to the task of clearing the ivy from around Polperro's family trees. In-breeding, which had been encouraged by the isolation of the village, had increased the complexity of most families 'haveage', the local word for lineage. The Minards family inspired Perrycoste to write 'I have this year spent an immense amount of time and trouble over this large family, and in the end I altered all the baptismal records over a long series of years from both Talland and Launceston in order to clear up a hopeless muddle.'

Things went from bad to worse and it must have seemed to Perrycoste that certain families had set out deliberately to foil any such enquiry. Of the Barretts he wrote 'Two men of the same name had a diabolical knack (as in other families) of marrying women of the same name.' If anyone actually went so far as to inbreed just to complicate matters, it must have been at a price. There is a legend that Richard Rowett, when tree-cutting one day, sat the wrong side of his saw and fell to a not too intelligent end.

'The purely individual peculiarities leave little or no visible trace;
the outline of the composite is the average of all the components.'

3 COMPOSITES OF CRIMINALS TAKEN FROM
4, 9 & 5, DIFFERENT PERSONS RESPECTIVELY, AND THE
CO-COMPOSITE OF THE WHOLE 18 OF THEM IN THE CENTRE.

5 LIKENESSES OF NAPOLEON I TAKEN AT DIFFERENT PERIODS
AND THE COMPOSITE OF THEM IN THE CENTRE.

The majority of Sir Francis Galton's work was concerned with
heredity, but two sidelines to this interest occupied him for several
years. On the first, fingerprinting, he published a book and
developed a system of classification which formed the basis of
today's computerised criminal files. On the second, composite
portraiture, (the combining of many different portraits into a
single resultant image), he produced several lengthy papers.

Galton's interests usually involved 'fairly simple mathematical
investigation with mechanical invention and experiment, but were
also closely associated with psychological and heredity enquiries.'
Composite photography, for which he devised some intricate
equipment, proved no exception. As he developed better systems
of combining separate portraits, so he began to apply the idea to a
greater range of subjects. In 1878 he spoke to the Antrhopological
Institute on 'Composite Portraits'. 'They give us typical pictures of
different races of men, if derived from a large number of
individuals of those races taken at random.' A year later he
delivered a lecture to the Royal Institute of Great Britain entitled
'Generic Images', in which he explained how memory works like a
composite, or generic, portrait.
'A generic mental image may be considered to be nothing more
than a generic portrait stamped on the brain by the successive

impressions made by its component images . . . The criterion of a perfect mind would lie in its capacity of always creating images of a truly generic kind, deduced from the whole range of its past experiences.'

In 1881, speaking to The Royal Photographic Society on 'Composite Portraiture' he suggested 'Young and old persons of both sexes can be combined into one ideal face. I can well imagine a fashion setting in to have these pictures.'

Finally he published 'An enquiry into the physiognomy of phthisis by the method of composite photography', carried out in 1881. This included a composite portrait formed of no less than 200 'unselected cases of phthisis.'

Apart from superimposing skulls for anthropological research (Thompson) and combining signatures to detect forgery (Frazer) composite photography led nowhere, (though identikit pictures are a modern relative). This was partly because of the laboriousness of the process and because it soon became clear that there was no apparent link between facial features and intellect.

Galton was later to use the fingerprints of Polperro fishermen for his researches into ways of classifying types. It is perhaps poetic that Harding had photographed the fathers of those same fishermen in the very way that Galton required for his work on composite photography. Maybe there exists in some attic a faded print of a composite fisherman wearing a generic hat. But it is hardly possible, for there is a difference between Galton's 'science' of groups and Harding's concern with the individual, for each of these eighty-two fishermen is named.

'The whole duty of the existence of creatures appears to be to draw nutrition, propagate and rot.'   J. Couch, 1847.

Relating Harding's photographs to his rookery diary might seem a little laboured, but it serves to show in one glance his entire work. Perhaps the way in which he observed the rookery was even similar to how he saw Polperro — the photographs being an extension of his rook eye. As well as containing roughly a thousand individuals each, the two gregarious communities had a number of things in common. Besides, just as mankind is hopelessly anthropormorphic, so probably are other creatures. As W.H. Hudson wrote in 1898, to the rook 'We are nothing but bigger rooks, somewhat mis-shapen, perhaps featherless, deprived by some accident of the faculty of flight, and not very well able to take care of ourselves.'

21st November
'Clustered in small and silent groups.'

26th February

'A very stormy night — at times blowing a hurricane — reported that the tide washed over Polperro bridge — a boat or two damaged, a man drowned, the women crying. The Rooks left at an early hour and one by one as it were striving against the wind which blows from the south west — At 3.00 p.m. many rooks came in and remained gloomily and silently on the trees.'

27th February

'We hear of the revolution in France, and that Louis Philipe has abdicated. The moral storm has its counterpart in the physical storms prevailing here. Since the last week the gales and squalls interfere with the rooks building their nests, they depart in the morning singly and gloomily, contending with the south wester. Storm continues to rage. Wind south west. We hear Louis Philipe is at Neuilly on his way here on the whirlwind which distresses these rooks.'

6th November

' — sometimes one seems to dig out of the grass something which
he carries to his mate and appears to feed her. They bow and
scrape at each other, and bring their bills in contact. Sometimes
when one has found something the other comes and takes it, like
chickens called by the hen when she has found anything —
generally among the pairs it is easy to distinguish one smaller than
the other, the larger probably the male. Sometimes when one has
found anything the other comes and takes it away forcibly.

Sometimes after two have been together for some time, a third
has got near and brought his bill in contact with one of the two as
if kissing after which he will go and drive the other away who will
make no resistance, but walk off — they seem to pick up a great
deal on the grass and swallow large mouthfuls of something, I
know not what.'

28th October

'From what I hear I begin to think all these sharp notes that are
heard are the cry of the jackdaw and not the rook, that the rook
has but a broad and hoarse voice and that the sharp one is the
jackdaw's. I observed again seven or eight of these jackdaws (like
half grown rooks) feeding on the grass. They keep to themselves
while feeding and although they go with the rooks in taking flight,
and roost with them, I think they have a tendency generally not to
be far from each other. One alone is not seen among the rooks,
but there will always be a few in company.'

This photograph shows Couch on the road leading down into Polperro. Sir Arthur Quiller-Couch remembered his grandfather as tall and upright as he 'strode his domain as its unchallengable great man, in top hat, high white stock, long black coat, and until past middle age, black breeches and silver buckled shoes — a costume which forfeited no dignity as he would sit, after his wont, on an inverted fish basket by the quay, with brush and paint-box ready and the eye of an osprey on the nets, should perchance they discharge something rare, however minute.'

4th November
'He looked very singular among his black companions, to be thus distinguished, the only one with extremities of wings white. I am informed that one similar was shot some years ago here, and stuffed by Mr. Jackson of Looe. If so this peculiarity must have been propagated and we may always expect to see one or two in the rookery of the singular appearance of this one.'

5th November
'. . . in going against the squall they don't advance direct against the wind, but slightly on one side then back to the other and help themselves on as much with the wind (on the principle of the ships advancing within a few points of the wind) as with our own muscular effort and they keep themselves sideways just sufficiently that the wind should not ruffle their feathers, as the helmsman manages to keep the sails taught, whenever so little more to the wind the sails would flap.'

29th October

'At 4.00 p.m. — all at home, ranged like divisions and companies
on the tops of the trees which extend in a circuit whose arc may
be a quarter of a mile measure, which they blackened as with a
dark fringe extending the whole length, they were stationary and
silent for a good while, with the exception of some always flying
here and there. Then they arose nearly all together and whirled in
the air sporting for some time, again they perched as before, again
rose in companies — always with noise in rising and in the air —'

15th May

'More shooting. Again after a lull in the storm of firing all the old
and young stand on the tops of the trees all directed towards the
point where the danger appears — all in animate conversation and
as if waiting for some new explosion — loud conversation and
intent looks in one direction resembles the crowd during a
political revolution, listening to the speeches of their leaders.
Sometimes applauding and then crying 'down, down' such a one,
they all seem determined upon some end by one means, others by
another, when the military appear and the conflict engages.
Dispersed in one quarter they appear in another in tenfold
numbers, and more clamorous than ever. Their homes are forsaken
— their domestic duties in abeyance — children follow after the
crowd and wives sob and cry and mothers deplore their losses and
still the confusion ceases not, but the battle cry, and the banners
and procession moves onwards — still disappears and reappears.
Nothing is heard in every direction but the clamour of war and the
accents of distress of hundreds — confusion, dust and heat and
blood overspreads the plain.'

3rd November
'Two rooks together on a branch playing and fighting for a twig which one holds in its bill.'

'During one of his long vacations, whilst botanizing around Trelawne, he (Jonathan) came upon Sir Harry standing lost in thought in the middle of the road. Just disappearing around the corner was an old woman heavily laden with a huge bundle of sticks. On young Couch making his presence known Sir Harry looked up and said, 'Well! I never had such a blow in my life before! I have often forbidden that old soul to pick sticks *out* of the fences, she may pick them *up* if she likes; just now I threatened to put my whip about her if I caught her at it again, and what do you think she tells me?'

'Something pithy, no doubt,' replied Couch.

'Just this,' says Sir Harry, 'Pooh! 'Tis only a *breath,* and 'tis as much mine as 'tis thine,' so I think I had better let her alone for the future,' and he did. For the rest of her life the old woman was allowed to pick *out* or pick *up* sticks, where and when she pleased; not a keeper on the estate was permitted to interfere with her.'

Life of Jonathan Couch, Bertha Couch, 1891.

5th March
'They select their sticks also, with some nicety, picking and choosing.'

4th November
'They generally stand basking in the sun motionless and silent.'

18th May
'Birds again feeding their young who receive food from their parents flapping their wings all the while and screeching — some are still·sitting on their young, who are not yet come out of the nest.'

29th April
'Some few young ones appear ready to come out of their nests.'

3rd November
'Many of the rooks seem two and two perched together — one is pecking at the head of his companion who seems to sit quietly to be thus pecked at, as if his companion were rendering him a service — this lasts about a minute.'

5th November
'Some shake their feathers and stretch out their wings as if yawning.'

6th November
'A jackdaw alights on a sitting sheep while three others are around him. The sheep's only notice of him is to wag his tail. The jackdaw runs along his back, gets upon his head and there stands, while another, just under the sheep's nose, looks up at him. By and by he hops on his head. Meanwhile the sheep remains quite quiet and while pecked at on the forehead, merely wags his tail.

Again a jackdaw alights on a sheep feeding. The sheep merely raises his head and stops feeding, remaining as still as a dog pointing, while the jackdaw rests on his head and pecks at his face. On the jackdaw leaving, the sheep resumes his posture.'

30th March
'. . . majority sitting on their nests.'

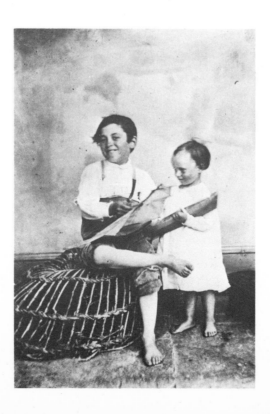

9th March
'The jackdaws particularly have kept up a concert for more than
an hour.'

3rd November
'A flock of them descend on the grass — four stray rooks come in from various directions.'

9th September
'There they chattered and bustled and fought for places with all the noise and clatter of a bevy of parrots and cockatoos in the bush.'

8th May
'Some of the young are seen occasionally standing on the edge of the nest.'

5th November
'Frequently two will stand together almost motionless for a length
of time.'

18th April
'If anyone attempted to lay out sticks in imitation of these nests, their work must have been blown down. A proof of the superior art with which they are built by the birds.'

10th March
'One nest that appeared in the morning a large old nest broken through and abandoned, now a bottom has been weaved across the ring and a rook is at work on it.'

An old lady remembered going down the street in Polperro and hearing nothing but the click clack of the knitting needles. Although Jonathan Couch lamented the fact that Polperro mended yet did not make its own nets, perhaps it was because the women were too busy making 'jersey frocks'. Girls learnt to knit when they were very young and soon their fingers 'would go so fast you could not see them.' But speed was not the only factor. The design across the shoulders and chest varied considerably and, as the discovery of these photographs has revealed, a greater variety of patterning existed than was suspected. With the aid of a magnifying glass Mary Wright of Launceston is knitting back the past.

Such pictures can reveal a wealth of information to the careful researcher, but it is possible to be misled. Francis Frith took the lower left photograph of Polperro and found it a little dull, so he borrowed the fishwife from a picture he had taken of Newlyn and transplanted her into the Polperro scene. Frith's pictorial considerations overrode any concern for historical accuracy, and the fact that Polperro had no need of fishwives was of no importance.

J. Valentine c.1890

From the 1880's onwards Polperro attracted itinerant amateur photographers, as well as professionals like Valentine and Frith who were covering Cornwall for their expanding postcard concerns. It is interesting to compare their later more picturesque views, taken with wider angle lenses, to Harding's more clustered scenes. While Hughes and Valentine positioned their distant figures to give scale, Harding's often play a more prominent part in the composition. The coastguard's telescope slants with the pier and hills and the frieze-like figures in the picture below complement the mast and its shadow.

H. Hughes 1904

How much this difference between the early and later works is due to a difference in outlook is questionable. Because he was using the wet-plate process, Harding made sure his effort was not wasted and consequently took a lot of trouble over setting up his figures. Hughes and Valentine did not know the locals well enough to organize them, as did Harding, furthermore they were probably only in Polperro for a day or so. As Perrycoste wrote in a letter to Galton in July 1903 explaining why it was taking him so long to collect the fingerprints: 'At this time of year the fishermen are usually in bed or at sea, and the only chance is to catch them at meal times or so, and this often involves half a dozen visits to catch one man, similarly school children have to be caught just after school and before they have vanished to play.'

'The artist has also found us out, and in the sketching season we get many painters of repute. Old Sam Cook has never tired of it and Hook stayed some time here painting the sturdy fishermen and their boats.'

Thomas Q. Couch, Mid-1870's?

The development of early photography in Britain could be shown quite successfully if one had only the work produced in four fishing villages — Hill and Adamson's calotypes of Newhaven, Harding's wet-plates of Polperro, Sutcliffe's dry-plates of Whitby and the huge quantity of pictures taken of St. Ives at the end of the dry-plate era. Probably much of the best British genre photography lies in these places.

Newhaven   Polperro   Whitby   St. Ives

Although St. Ives was much larger and less isolated than Polperro — consequently attracting painters and tourists at an early date — there are no photographs of Harding's vintage. At St. Ives, as was more often the case, photographers followed in the path of the painters.

J. Douglas

Not long before these two photographs were taken, the St. Ives fishing industry was in its heyday and seagulls thrived on an abundance of fish. But as soon as the massive pilchard shoals began to decline gulls started to move inland, later forsaking the cliffs to nest on rooftops and in a few rare cases to set up home in trees!

W.H. Lanyon

In 1959 for example a pair of herring gulls nested in a pine at St. Austell, though they produced no young. The negative illustration of this occasion is a copy of a transparency sent to the Truro Museum and accentuates the strangeness of the scene.

This general move inland has had other spectacular side effects and in St. Ives recently the public gardens had to be closed during nesting time after some gardeners had been forced to defend themselves with broomsticks. But it is not only the seagulls that are changing their habits. In 1975 a rook count was held in Cornwall and revealed a 30% decline in the total rook population since the last war. We know from Harding's diary that in 1847 there were 478 nests at Trelawne whereas today there are only a handful.

As Couch noted in 1847 rooks will only 'nest in the neighbourhood of some dignified mansion.' One such mansion, Trelawne, is not what it was. Nests for a thousand birds are today nests for as many holiday-makers and the birdbath is a heated swimming pool.

10th December
'5.00 p.m. Dark and no rooks arrived! — First time since this journal began that the rooks have failed to return. They have always returned at least an hour before dark, today I know not what has become of them, they have not been seen in the neighbourhood . . .'